HOLLYWOOD ISLE

Catalina Island Picture Book

Mini Coffee Table Book

Welcome

HOLLYWOOD'S MAGICAL ISLAND-CATALINA THROUGH THE REMARKABLE EYE of first time film director, GREG REITMAN, we get a first hand glimpse of the images that made the historical documentary of Catalina Island. The story begins with the acquisition of the Santa Catalina Island Company in 1919 led by William Wrigley, Jr. He set a course for Catalina's future in the world of art, sports, music, and entertainment that was unmatched in US history, even through present day.

One of William Wrigley Jr. first ventures was the creation of the Sugarloaf Casino. This octagonal, steel framed, stud and stucco structure, with two wings for concessions, was completed in 1920, at a cost of $250,000. In 1928, the Sugarloaf Casino was dismantled to make way for a new Casino on the same site. The steel framework of the Sugarloaf Casino was moved to Avalon Canyon, becoming the world's largest single birdcage. From inside the "Bird Park" tourists could view thousands of birds of all colors, sizes, and temperaments from around the world.

One day in the early 1920's William Wrigley, Jr. and David Malcolm Renton, his Vice President and General Manager, were up in the Catalina Canyon where they found themselves stuck in one of the clay deposits. Out of this accidental monumental discovery was born a tile and brick factory at Pebbly Beach in 1927. Throughout the town of Avalon the Catalina tile are present in the form of Catalina Blue, Tonyon Red, Descano Green, and Manchu Yellow. Present Catalina tile sites include, the façade at Catalina Crafters, The El Encanto, the Planter in the Island Plaza, and CC Gallagher's. The tile designs are generally birds, seascapes or sea creatures. For years, Catalina tile and pottery were popular throughout the world and they are now highly collectible. The factory closed down in 1937.

William Wrigley, Jr. and his advertising partner, Otis Shepard, drew up plans to market the Island to the world. Transportation was critical to the commercial success of the island. William Wrigley, Jr. expanded the fleet by adding two new vessels: the SS Avalon in 1921 and the SS Catalina in 1924. For the next 50 years, the SS Catalina escorted more than 25 million passengers to the Island. As the steamers headed into the pier, "Miss Catalina" speedboats guided them in. At the pier, passengers would throw coins into the water for

local divers to retrieve. For more prosperous people, small excursion packages offered discount packages to fly in on the seaplane-Curtis F flying boats.

William Wrigley, Jr. and his staff were committed to creating, in Avalon, a place of unlimited and extraordinary bounty. Under the tutelage of master builder, David Renton, it would take only fourteen months to unveil Catalina most beloved treasure, the Catalina Casino.

On May 29, 1929, at a cost of over $2 million dollars the Catalina Casino was unveiled to the world. The Casino building stands 140 feet high with a diameter of 178 feet with the encircling loggia measuring 14 feet wide and 8 feet high. The ballroom is 158 feet in diameter with 15,000 square feet of dance floor making it the "world's largest circular ballroom."

After seeing a sketch prepared on two days notice, Mr. Wrigley hired John Gabriel Beckman to create the murals for the Casino. Beckman's design evolved from an original Greek theme to reflect the underwater surroundings of the new Casino. At the entrance of the theatre, the first series of the Beckman murals are nine 10 X 25 panels, encircling he walls of the loggia. These murals are underwater scenes of colorful stylized marine life floating against a green background. The central motif is that of the mermaid directly over the ticket booth along with sea horses in brilliant colors with schools of fish, kelp, blue crabs, purple lobsters, and other aquatic life. Beckman designed the original murals to be executed in glazed Catalina tile. In the rush to complete the building, the scenes were painted directly onto the concrete surface. In 1986, tile artist Richard Keit with the help of John Gabriel Beckman, who was then 88 years old, created the mermaid scene in tile.

Inside the Avalon Theatre, theatergoers pass through glass doors to find themselves in a foyer paneled with 4,500 board feet of black walnut measuring 12 feet high with a beamed barrel fresco ceiling of corral-red shot with golden stars. The theater auditorium has a diameter of 138 feet and a 43-foot-high ceiling, coupled with a 44-foot by 24-foot proscenium arch defining the stage. The original seating capacity was 1,250. The Catalina Casino was also the first theatre in the world built for sound pictures, and in tests, the acoustics have proven perfect. In 1931, the Casino design was utilized in the building of the Radio City Music Hall in New York City.

The Opening of the Catalina Casino launched the Golden Age and the Big Band era. Many of the great acts played on Catalina including Dick Jurgens, Benny Goodman, Glenn Miller, Buddy Rogers, Kay Kyser, Bob Crosby, Woody Herman, Stan Kenton, and the famous Les Brown and "His Band of Renown." Weeknight crowds often included 3,000 people. Admission charges to the ballroom ran from $.25 on the weeknights to $.40 on weekends.

The establishment of the Catalina Casino also brought in the Hollywood community. Producers, directors, writers, actors, singers, studio executives all flocked to get a taste of paradise. Humphrey Bogart, Stan Laurel, Olive Hardy, Al Jolsen, Orsen Welles, John Wayne, Johnny Weismuller, Charlie Chaplin, Zane Grey, Jimmy Durante, Errol Flynn, Cary Grant, Clark Gable, Robert Wagner, Natalie Wood, Jackie Cooper, Jean Harlow, Dolores Del Rio, Paulette Goddard, Mickey Rooney, Gloria Swanson, and Bonita Granville, all made Avalon there second home.

Catalina also became a favorite spot for filmmakers and studios, evident in the number of motion pictures produced on the island. An estimated two hundred and fifty films were filmed on the Island. Among the films include "Chinatown," "Mutiny on the Bounty," "Treasure Island," "Old Ironsides," "The Buccaneer," "The Glass Bottom Boat," and "Jaws," to name a few.

In addition, some of the top agencies sent their models on photo shoots to the island. Adding to the allure of the so-called "Romance Island", Leighton Noble formed the "Miss Catalina Swimsuit Company" and charted the "SS Avalon" to bring patrons to a private showing of the swimsuit line that featured eighty models.

Beginning in 1921, William Wrigley Jr's 'Chicago Cubs' enjoyed the paradise splendor by spending the next 30 years of spring training on Catalina Island. The first season only the pitchers and catchers were brought for conditioning, but in later years, the entire team came. A baseball stadium was constructed adjacent to the golf course. During the thirty-year era, Wrigley Cubs featured talent from baseball legends

Honus Wagner, Joseph McCarthy, Dizzy Dean, Phil Cavaretto, and even launched Ronald Reagan's acting career, bringing him over as the official sports cast announcer.

Like many vacation paradises, Catalina had its decline. World War II led Catalina to shift from a tourist destination to a military base. With the bombing of Pearl Harbor, on December 7, 1941, the bright lights of Catalina were blacked out. Norma Jean Baker, eventually becoming Marilyn Monroe, also lived on the island during this time, and married James Dougherty, her first husband. Mr. Dougherty trained in Avalon with the US Maritime Service and when he got his first permanent assignment, it was an instructor in Avalon. Norma Jean then joined him on the island. She was often seen spending her days near the bird park or strolling along the beaches.

After William Wrigley, Jr.'s death in 1932, his son, Philip Knight Wrigley, continued to develop the island. Though tremendous pressure was put on P.K. Wrigley to sell the island or develop it, he felt strongly as had his father before him, that Catalina should retain its natural beauty for future generations.

In 1972, "The Santa Catalina Island Conservancy" was created as a "non profit" foundation charged with preserving the Island's scenic beauty and open spaces. "Geographic Conservancy Spots" were set-up throughout the island as a means for preservation. One particular site, the Wrigley Botanical Garden, preserves the six endemic plant species found nowhere else on the planet. These species include: 'Trask's Mahogany', 'St. Catherine's Lace', 'Catalina Manzanita', 'Catalina Ironwood', 'Santa Catalina Bedstraw', and Catalina Dudleya.

Another geological spot is the Jacques Cousteau Monument, an underwater preservation park positioned directly below the Casino Point. This entire island is covered with an abundance of flora and fauna, sea life, giant kelp forests, Santa Catalina island fox, beechey ground squirrel, Santa Catalina island deer mouse, Santa Catalina island harvest mouse, Santa Catalina island shrew, Bewick's wren, California quail, Hutton's vireo. More importantly, the island's ecological system is intact and supports the protection of the bald eagle, and more than 1,000 species of marine plants and animals, including dolphins, seals, whales, sea lions, buffalo, and millions of individual organisms.

Development of the Island

William Wrigley, Jr. Born 1861 Died 1932

Philip Knight Wrigley
Laying Out Downtown Avalon, 1934

Crescent Avenue, Avalon, Transformed, 1934

William Wrigley, Jr Home, "Mt. Ada"

Catalina Golf Course

Philip K. Wrigley Home, "Casa Del Monte"

D.M. Renton, Ranch Manager, William Wrigley, Jr and J.H. Partrick, 1922

Downtown Beach

Sugarloaf Bird Park

The Original Curator with a Mccaw Bird

Flock of Flamingos

Inside the World's "Largest Bird Cage"

Two Toucans with the Curator

Entering the Bird Park, 1928

Pebbly Beach and the Tile

Women Showcasing the Pottery

Pebbly Beach, 1920's

Sombrero Fountain

Catalina Smart Luncheon Set

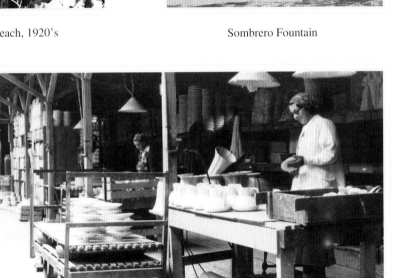

Tile Production Line

Catalina Pottery Shop Interior

Casino Construction

Casino Construction, 1928

Catalina Casino, 1929

Beckman Murals

John Gabriel Beckman

John Beckman's and Richard Keit's
Final Tile Design

Modern Casino Mermaid

Original Casino Mermaid

Fresco Mural

Fresco Mural

Wrigley Steamers

"S.S. Catalina" and "S.S. Avalon" in Avalon Bay

The "S.S. Catalina" entering Avalon Bay

The Officers of the Ship

The Mariachis

Leaving Los Angeles Harbor for Catalina Island

Passengers Disembarking

Coin Divers

Passengers Throwing Coins

Diver's Eye View

Diver's Catching Coins

Storing Their Coins

Counting Their Loot

Amphibian Planes

The Captains

Mooring at the St. Catherine Hotel

First Water to Water Seaplane Landing,
May 10, 1912, by Glenn Martin

Glenn Martin 25th Anniversary

Hamilton Cove, Catalina's First Airport

Seaplane Landing in Avalon Bay

Big Bands

"Welcome Gordon Clan!"

"The Four Preps"
Composed "26 Miles Across The Sea"

Big Band Legend Milton Hearth

Dancing in the Casino Ballroom

Freddy Martin

Herbie Kay and Jan Garber

Big Bands

Les Brown Orchestra

Kay Kyser, Playing to the Largest Crowd in the History of the Casino, 6200 Dancers, June 1940

Dick Jurgens Orchestra

Kay Kyser Shaking Hands with Benny Goodman

Benny Goodman and his Orchestra

Celebrities

Bonita Granville and Jackie Cooper

Dolores Del Rio and Orson Welles

Henry Fonda

Johnny Weismuller

Charlie Chaplin and Paulette Goddard

Celebrities

Olive Hardy and Stan Laurel with their Wives

Errol Flynn

Winston Churchill

Robert Wagner and Natalie Wood

Humphrey Bogart

Jimmy Durante

The Movies

Movies Come to the Island

John Ford's "Bucaneer"

Cecil B. DeMille's "Feet Of Clay"

Jackie Cooper in "Treasure Island"

Entering the Casino Theatre

The Starlets

Peggy Moran

Helen Parish

Dorothy Darrell

Three Models

Kathryn Adams Sitting on the Tile

A Starlet at the "St. Catherine Hotel"

Swimsuit Models

"Miss Catalina Swimsuit Contest"

Model in the "Arch Casino Way"

Models with the Flying Fish

Models on the "Plaza Fountain"

Two Archer Models

Models on the Beach

Models on beach at the "St. Catherine Hotel"

Glamour Girls

Models "Aquaplaning"

Two Models at Descanso Beach

Two Models Aquaplaning

Model on a Surfboard

Miss Catalina 5

Cubs

Ronald Reagan Sportscast Announcer for the
"Cubs" Spring Training in Avalon, 1936-1937

Cubs Ballpark on Catalina Island

Chicago Cubs disembarking off the "S.S. Catalina"

Philip Knight Wrigley with Phil Cavaretto

Cubs Practicing

William Wrigley Jr. with the Cubs

Norma Jean Baker

Norma Jean dreaming of being an Actress

Norma Jean with her First Husband James Dougherty at the Pier

Norma Jean and James Dougherty at the Bird Park

Norma Jean Baker and James Dougherty Wedding Picture

Preservation Of The Island

Philip Knight Wrigley

Cactus Fields

Shark Harbor

Wrigley Botanical Gardens

The Sea Lions

The North American Bison

The Cactus Garden

Modern Day Catalina Island

The Casino Way

Holly Hill House

The Beach

The Metropole Marketplace

The Dinghy Dock

Antonio's

The Catalina Express

Sunset at Little Harbor

Backside of the Island, Shark and Little Harbor